Circles Where the Head Should Be

Previous Winners of the Vassar Miller Prize in Poetry
Scott Cairns, Founding Editor
John Poch, Series Editor

Partial Eclipse by Tony Sanders
Selected by Richard Howard

Delirium by Barbara Hamby
Selected by Cynthia Macdonald

The Sublime by Jonathan Holden
Selected by Yusef Komunyakaa

American Crawl by Paul Allen
Selected by Sydney Lea

Soul Data by Mark Svenvold
Selected by Heather McHugh

Moving & St rage by Kathy Fagan
Selected by T. R. Hummer

A Protocol for Touch by Constance Merritt
Selected by Eleanor Wilner

The Perseids by Karen Holmberg
Selected by Sherod Santos

The Self as Constellation by Jeanine Hathaway
Selected by Madeline DeFrees

Bene-Dictions by Rush Rankin
Selected by Rosanna Warren

Losing and Finding by Karen Fiser
Selected by Lynne McMahon

The Black Beach by J. T. Barbarese
Selected by Andrew Hudgins

re-entry by Michael White
Selected by Paul Mariani

The Next Settlement by Michael Robins
Selected by Anne Winters

Mister Martini by Richard Carr
Selected by Naomi Shihab Nye

Ohio Violence by Alison Stine
Selected by Eric Pankey

Stray Home by Amy M. Clark
Selected by Beth Ann Fennelly

CIRCLES
WHERE THE HEAD
SHOULD BE

POEMS BY
CAKI WILKINSON

2010 WINNER, VASSAR MILLER PRIZE IN POETRY

UNIVERSITY OF NORTH TEXAS PRESS
DENTON, TEXAS

10 9 8 7 6 5 4 3 2 1

Permissions:
University of North Texas Press
1155 Union Circle #311336
Denton, TX 76203-5017

The paper used in this book meets the minimum requirements of the
American National Standard for Permanence of Paper for Printed
Library Materials, z39.48.1984. Binding materials have been chosen for
durability.

Library of Congress Cataloging-in-Publication Data

Wilkinson, Caki, 1980-
Circles where the head should be :
poems / by Caki Wilkinson. -- 1st ed.
p. cm. -- (Number 18 in the Vassar Miller prize in poetry series)
Vassar Miller Prize in Poetry, 2010
ISBN 978-1-57441-309-0 (pbk. : alk. paper)
I. Title. II. Series: Vassar Miller prize in poetry series ; no. 18.
PS3623.I553C57 2011
811'.6--dc22

2010043126

Circles Where the Head Should Be is Number 18
in the Vassar Miller Prize in Poetry Series

Cover illustration *Chamonix* is by Ian Carpenter. Used by permission.

For my parents

CONTENTS

III.

ACKNOWLEDGMENTS

Acknowledgment is made to the following publications for poems that first appeared in them, sometimes in slightly different form.

32 Poems: "Shaping Behaviors"
American Poetry Journal: "Girl Under Bug Zapper"
The Atlantic: "Bower Bird"
Birmingham Poetry Review: "Mnemosyne," "*Ecce Signum*!" "Involution" and "Offices"
Black Warrior Review: "Fisher King"
Cincinnati Review: "Miniatures"
Measure: "Dead Matter"
Oxford American: "Genealogy" and "Itinerant"
Poetry: "Cosmogony" and "Lares and Penates"
Raintown Review: "Women's Studies"
Sewanee Theological Review: "Bildungsroman"
Smartish Pace: "Assisted Living," "The Truth About Distance"
Southwest Review: "A Correlated History of Synchronicity"
Unsplendid: "Lady on a Unicycle"
Yale Anthology of Younger American Poetry (forthcoming): "Bower Bird," "Cosmogony," "Girl Under Bug Zapper" and "Lady on a Unicycle"
Yale Review: "Storm and Stress"
Verse Daily (reprints): "Fisher King" and "Lady on a Unicycle"

I would like to thank Johns Hopkins University, the University of Cincinnati, and the Poetry Foundation for supporting me with generous fellowships.

Many thanks as well to the directors, cast, and crew of the Sewanee Writers' Conference, and to my teachers and friends, who so often are one and the same.

The one thing which we seek with insatiable desire is to forget ourselves, to be surprised out of our propriety, to lose our sempiternal memory, and to do something without knowing how or why; in short, to draw a new circle.

—Ralph Waldo Emerson

I.

COSMOGONY

A ball of yarn, a hill
maintain an equipoise until
    their neatness starts to bore the gods
        of potential and energy
    who hedge bets, reckoning the odds
        of when the rest will be

set in motion, and who,
first stumbling upon this clew,
    constructed both the incline and
        the inclination to unwind.
    Like most gods, though, they haven't planned
        to stay; they mastermind

the scheme, *ex nihilo,*
then slip behind the shadow show
    and designate an agent, chief,
        remaker of their mischief made.
    Each time, disguised, this leitmotif
        gets salvaged and replayed,

a universe begins,
for orogens and origins
    suppose a Way Things Were before
        some volatile, untimely That—
    sweetness perverted by the core
        or the belfry by the bat,

or here, a hilly green,
whose still life, eerily serene,
    completes their best contrivance yet:
        from high above, a williwaw,
    a hiss, and then the silhouette
        of one terrific paw.

LARES AND PENATES

The suburbs? Well, for heaven's sake
who wouldn't choose the absolute
convenience? Cheap, a quick commute,
and close to Lowe's, a Steak and Shake,
our own police and DMV,
    a library, a lake.

Esteemed domestic diplomats,
we trump conundrums (His and Hers)
and smother any fuss that stirs
the air of habit-habitats.
It's not an easy job; in short,
    we wear a lot of hats.

Our curb's appealing. From the street
you'd miss the issues we're ignoring:
termites and week-old dishes mooring,
barnacled with shredded wheat,
the bunch of brown bananas stuck
    with a yellow Post-It: *Eat!*

We dictate chores, but understand
the clock moves faster than we do
and focus on those old and blue
dilemmas of the second hand:
inheritance, ill-fitting pants,
    smoke, rumors, foreclosed land.

Winters, we help keep track of taxes,
sort copies Xerox-hot in piles,
or prune unruly hanging files
(a fixture of our weekend praxis).
There's always something. In this house,
    only the cat relaxes—

4

because the clutter drives a need
for more, more room, more hours, food,
more faith in the subjunctive mood...
tomorrow, yes, we should succeed
in keeping peace and making time
     to garden, and to read.

Still, every spring our porches spawn
insects we can't identify
and ferns turned freeze-dried octopi.
They spill into the arid lawn
with diasporic fliers, clover
     and choirs of woebegone

house sparrows whose incessant cheeping
recalls the gloomy *Ubi sunt,*
our soundtrack to the nightly hunt
for whatever is downstairs, beeping.
(As if the sleepless needed some
     reminder they're not sleeping.)

But don't fret; clarity, if brief,
is possible. With luck, you'll see
an artfulness in entropy—
the rust, the dust, the bas-relief
of Aquafresh-encrusted sinks.
     So when, in disbelief,

a woman skims new catalogs,
convinced her luster's fading, faded,
and, afraid to end up jaded,
doughy in orthotic clogs,
she gracefully accepts her fate
     and rises early. Jogs.

BOWER BIRD

Old news, the midnight warblers worrisome
to introspective bards, the nagging taps
and jugs that left so many haunted, dumb,

behind their coppice gates or chamber doors—
but witness, now, this feathered architect,
a bricoleur, exotic, who ignores

convention, working long before he sings
to gather fragile lumber, sticks and seeds,
although, part larcenist, his favorite things

come from the human world: milk caps or pairs
of pearly buttons once attached to tags;
matchsticks, cigar bands, red synthetic hairs

uprooted from some coconut baboon
or other Florabama souvenir,
stripped screws, receipts, even the jagged moon

of a fingernail blown, dusty, from the Hoover.
And steadfast to the finders keepers rule,
this passerine Houdini will maneuver

through apertures in transoms, cracks in attics,
encroaching on such odd forgotten hobbies
as medieval reenactments, numismatics

Hummels, and paint-by-numbers, hauling back
whatever he can muster, though he's less
a petty crook than kleptomaniac,

since unlike history's most famous thieves,
Prometheus and Charlie Peace, Capone
and Robin Hood, he's charmed by gingko leaves

the same as blazing gold, for he equates
the value of a find with how it fits
into the complex structure he creates.

Bizarre, this art through which he resurrects
a story of disjointed parts, the cause
extracted from his manifold effects—

call it a burnished hut, a self-made cage,
a bachelor pad; in fact, his bower's nothing
but a vehicle, the decorated stage

where he's transformed. The undisputed prince
of bric-a-brac, his solo trill persists
whether or not he has an audience,

the coda rocking walls designed to glisten
yet hardly strong enough to house his hope
those finest plumes, on their high perch, will listen.

LADY ON A UNICYCLE

Every body continues in its state of rest, or of uniform motion in a right line, unless it is compelled to change that state by forces impressed upon it.

—Newton's First Law

So Esse Pearl gets snowed in at the chichi condo
    of that married man she sees,
and—you can filter this however you think fit—
she's upstairs, toweling off burst-bubble film, her chest
    chafed from his monogram,
and *he's* shut in the parlor, leafing through sheet music—

but just the glockenspiel, he says, to swallow all
    the woodwinds in his head—
when, glancing towards the porch to contemplate a scale,
he sees a woman poised, it seems, above the fluff
    of shrubs before the sheer
pink streetlights show her high boots turn a single wheel.

Now here's the kicker: he goes back to reading, forgets
    even to mention it
until they take a holiday months later (months!),
like it wasn't worth writing home about—and *that's*
    the kind of man he is,
Esse Pearl says, a mess of grandioso themes

the rest of us can't hear; and (bless her heart) wrapped up
    in his wife's terrycloth,
she never knew what passed: a whistle-trill of spokes
turned over salted asphalt, the easy lean achieved
    by holding on to nothing,
the freedom of a body that can stop itself.

SAME LADY, DIFFERENT UNICYCLE

Reaching the metro station, soaked, galoshes
sloshing, commuters stop to empty things—
a hood, a tote—into the sidewalk grate;

the overhang ladles their hair with rain.
Bevies of wet umbrellas ruffle past.
They hurry underground, all trundling

the same dark luggage, and learn the Red Line north
is making only local stops. *Enough,*
they think: another morning's ticker tape

looped with bad news. Too soon, they've had enough.
Squinting through platform steam, they hate to wait,
heads spinning, phones flipped out like hands—*Back off,*

I'm searching for a signal—never mind
the squatter by the bottom stair who thrums
his old guitar. Hard to imagine how

one finds an opening through coats and ponchos,
but she does, this lady on a unicycle.
A child tugs his mother's sleeve, points, *Look!*

and they watch her thread the madding masses, drop
a dollar for the song, and pedal on,
tilted into the gray, available light.

THE TRUTH ABOUT EFFECTS

Hens form one of the minor tragedies of the floods.
                    —The Dearborn Independent, *June 1927*

There's hardly rhyme or reason for a flood
or what it swallows. Water rose in spurts,
then leveled everything. A gust of mud.

The lucky were called *spared*: they hadn't drowned
on rooftops. From high ground, some raised their shirts,
comparing watermarks; some made a mound

of salvage—heaped, but dry. *You had to choose,*
one man would say. He left his hens in runs
and hauled his father's anvil, which he'd use

to prop the basement door—though, like the levee,
he brought it up some nights, bestowed on sons
who found it unremarkable, but heavy.

GENEALOGY

It had to do with little leaden things,
a belt unbuckled, rumors, epithets
they tried and stuck with, their inheritance:
nearsightedness, short fuses, long regrets.

One said, you know, I'd hoped for more than this.
The other, why'd you think you get to hope?
It had to do with what they did, and didn't,
a mirror's smears, hair nested in the soap.

Out of this blinkered logic, they begot
the whole town's whispers. Spoken like a curse:
Knocked up. A waitress at the Dairy Maid
spread it (her second cousin was their nurse).

The baby, it was no surprise, grew up
on powdered milk, saltines, government cheese—
since lonely's poor is worse, she bore another,
as if bless-you was meant to cure a sneeze.

They tried. And stuck with their inheritance,
but not a lick of sense, they reinvested,
hell-bent to break the cycle, make ends meet.
She went to Junior College. He got arrested—

it had to do with what they did, and didn't.
One son took sides. The other never kept
a promise or a steady anything.
He quit the church league, grew a mustache, slept,

knocked up a waitress at the Dairy Maid.
Head Majorette, she twirled, but looked a wreck,
didn't return after the baby came,
the birth cord wound around its purple neck.

Since lonely's poor is worse, she bore another
and stole away to live with kin, her past
forgotten when she tied the knot again:
a man's man who hung on (unlike the last),

hell-bent to break the cycle, make ends meet;
who had AC, four boys, and dogs that hunted;
who strategized, ascending through the ranks
to hold his father's post. It's all she'd wanted:

a promise or a steady anything.
But children leave (tied down, sewn-up) a void,
the referent of needs no longer needed.
She caught a lump. Her husband, once deployed,

didn't return. After the baby came
(their last surprise), she left the bills and yard
she couldn't face (his legacy, or hers?),
skipped town, and cropped him from the Christmas card,

forgotten. When she tied the knot again,
she framed the news; her new man worked with solder
and flux—their life: clippings, *memento mori*
turned paperweights, stepsons, a whip-smart daughter

who strategized, ascending through the ranks;
who read *Theogony*, said *autodidact*,
sought refuge in big-city-life—but driven
to get a job with benefits, got carjacked.

The referent of needs no longer needed?
Husband. Too soon, she wished she'd never married.
It had to do with little leaden things,
the fumes a body runs on, grudges carried.

She couldn't face his legacy—or hers,
it seemed—and, scotched, they opted for a gloss.
One said, you know, I'd hoped for more than this,
but there it was, refulgent in the dross

and flux—their life: clippings, *memento mori*
assembled like a line nobody drew
out of this blinkered logic. They begot
a tough, bow-legged brood. The middle two

sought refuge in big-city life, but driven
to bouts of rage, found mediocrity.
The baby, it was no surprise, grew up
sore as the dickens, hating kids. Had three.

GIRL UNDER BUG ZAPPER

This haywire night, she's back from church
    with neighbors, plain-faced Pentecostal types
whose scowls cut through the windshield's smears
    when her door slammed, no *thank you ma'am* or wave,

who'd still be scowling, could they see
    she kowtows on rotten boards, the porch suffused
with purple-blues no regal soul
    would praise, to maim a wayward gypsy moth.

She likes to watch them die, the stunned
    and stunted, slugs betrayed by falling salt,
cicadas gutted, anthills razed
    like circus grounds after a hurricane,

and while a kinder child might stray
    from incantations, cataclysmic winds
of aerosol, or soda froth,
    her heart's a mudcake shrunken in the sun.

Besides, she's seen enough of them
    hooked onto eaves and storm doors, dull as leaves,
and knows they'll drop, spun from the shock
    of pain, or rapture, creatures slain in spirit.

Besides, she'd rather celebrate
    the world unhinged, its crooked scales and stakes,
party-of-one who plucks these wings,
    confetti in her folded palms. Frail things.

PORTRAIT OF THE ARTIST
WITH TOOTHPICK BRIDGE

Last place: in retrospect, I could've thought
about the laws of Statics and Kinetics,
or drawn a blueprint. No, I chose aesthetics,
hung up, like all new kids, on first impressions.
But decorating sticks with sticks, I grew
concerned: my trusses barely bore the glue,
much less a brick. Poorly conceived, and wrought,

the thing was lucky it survived the ride
to school. And while I'd gain perspective, years
after I faced the junior engineers,
the meantime left me to my indiscretions:
minor, but of a very public nature.
Despite my having learned the nomenclature
of tension-turned-suspension, I relied

on other terms: an ornamental apse
and ziggurats, I said, were more my style.
Thus, holding it together for my trial
was difficult. I tried to make concessions
for shaky hands and braces, but fell short—
a lesson, not in how to build support,
but how to stand back, watching it collapse.

ITINERANT

He's driving, one hand down an Arby's sack,
and—Jesus Bleeping Christ—we're nowhere close,
sentenced to Kansas. Kansas: home of wheat,
the nation's largest prairie dog, and plains
that lend some credence to the pancake-world
hypothesis. I need to pee. Again.
You stick two people in an F-150
for three days, lugging pets and plants and far
more baggage than they're willing to admit,
their separate self-reflection starts to breed
apotheosis or abomination—
and usually the latter: we're both pissed.
Who died and made you king? I say. He says,
Sometimes your big mouth bites you in the ass,
and then he pegs me with a chicken finger—
not *at* me, *near* me, he'll maintain for weeks
after the incident, but either way,
it whips my left ear, hard, a deep-fried dart,
before it's sucked into the floorboard vortex,
that point of no return between our seats.

MNEMOSYNE

Mnemosyne, one must admit, has shown herself to be a very careless girl.

—Vladimir Nabokov

She's no spring chicken, lately too consumed
with baggage of her own, while yours, misplaced,
circles the great black hole of files erased.
She smokes too much, but keeps her wrists perfumed,

fanning a fragrance vaguely pickled, sweet,
and, unamused, her daughters scrunch their noses
at the whole charade, the floppy hats and poses
(by now, they've learned her rules are obsolete)—

because she chooses sides in arguments,
a trained conclusion jumper who disdains
gray areas in protocol and brains.
"Ask St. Anthony," she says, and circumvents

attempts to call up *ladyfingers, Dawn,*
and coffee…rubber gloves, white flour, while
a wrist gets misted in the produce aisle.
White ladyfingers, gloves, coffee, and Dawn…

and what else? *Doh.* Well, should've made a list.
Necessity's a bitch and lack evades
the logic of our best mnemonic aids
(like grade school sayings written to assist

with spectrums, treble clefs, and unsolved Xs,
the facts far less enduring than the fictions
of Roy G. Biv, Aunt Sally's dear afflictions).
So introduced to wormholes, googolplexes,

we're lost in space. The means becomes the end
just as a match, expired, lives in coals
that melt the wax of our impressioned souls
(a trickle down effect). We may pretend

some common truth exists, some central wick,
and yet, who really knows the way it was
in bygone lighting? Darling, no one does—
no one but you, a sandlot first-round pick

or former runner-up for Miss Teen Reno,
still signing notes with handles metonymic
of your only front-page feat, an ancient gimmick
like Homer's lines immortalizing Ino

for her slim ankles (—wait, what did she do?)
We're pressed to process, so we simplify,
ignoring how the process works, and why,
and Mnemosyne, the tart, fights déjà vu

again, a fallout having split her clan
since Clio's coming off the mania,
Erato's fine with boys, and Urania
has deep-sixed (ah! *dis*-aster) the cosmic plan

in favor of a more arresting story
where Pluto's booted, Venus overrated,
eclipsed by someone's very educated
mother, in all her culinary glory.

FISHER KING

They sold my favorite dive
    to Revco
the week my gangrene toes
    got clipped clean
(a logging accident—
    I sued, lost).
No doctor slipped me salve
    or sundries.
Crews trucked and gutted, adding
    fluorescent
lighting, a pharmacy,
    blood pressure
detectors, freezer cases.
    Stools were sawed
to kindling, and they boxed
    twelve dozen
pint glasses by the curb—
    a damn shame.
It's been some twenty years
    and counting,
but every day is bland
    as water.
I can't bring myself to try
    the pricey
uptown joints, and most evenings
    I return
to this familiar lot,
    stand outside
and watch the smocked employees
    locking up.
When the store goes black, glares
    from streetlights
reflect me still inside where,
    decades back,

I joined the other loggers
    after work,
slurping a dozen cold
    lobed oysters
with hot-sauce stinging low
    in my throat
while Johnny Carson beamed,
    all toothy,
"That's outstanding, really
    fabulous."
Now, approaching longer days,
    the patrons
come at sunset and linger
    past closing.
The spring aisle is tangled
    with windsocks
and women buying windsocks.
    I'm hungry
for one. She's young and yellow
    rain-slickered
like the Morton Salt girl,
    and I keep
a pearl under my tongue,
    lozenged there
in the grotto of my mouth,
    a flawless
specimen I've saved, waiting
    for the glossed
lips ready to receive it
    and heal me
through closeness, make my heavy
    boots buoyant.
This is modern medicine.
    This is me
corkscrewed through parting skies,
    the naked
seraphs crooning, *isn't it*
    fabulous?

BILDUNGSROMAN

We open with the girl, born premature
and blundersome (asthmatic, pigeon-toes,
a crooked nose)—hardly the cynosure
her genes could've produced. God only knows

what caused the mix-up, and why she won't take
her mother's milk, or cow's, but they agree
nutrition's crucial, and may make or break
her blossoming. They call her Peony,

and Kid, and though mostly a tragic spaz
(they blame this on an inner ear disorder),
she sees, in common junk, a raw pizzazz
that's worth preserving and, an avid hoarder,

builds shoebox reliquaries: dead bugs, pet
pebbles and shells, goose feathers, bits of string,
the last *matryoshka* stolen from a set,
some origami swans. That sort of thing.

Yet formal education marks the start
of something larger. *Driven by a motor*,
the doctors say. She says, I will be smart,
an astronaut or princess, so they quote her

in the monthly bulletin, adding, *Dream big!*
which resonates, a crucial turnabout:
for so long powered by the whirligig
of solitude, she seeks the world without.

(Reader, she has no choice. The records state
that most awakenings reflect this theme.)
And so, under the tutelage of great
and honorable broads, that all-star team

of social studies primers—Earhart, Arc,
Barton, Tubman, and Ross—she grasps the mold
she must grow into, nascent matriarch-
in-waiting. She earns A's, learns how to fold

a flag and fake a smile. She paints the walls
then crouches in her closet, double-jointed,
before a throng of catatonic dolls,
and says, "Girls, I'm not mad, just disappointed."

She takes up basketball (a perilous
but calculated act of self-reliance)
and challenges the boys who spit and cuss
and who've descended, she's convinced, from giants.

She campaigns for the lead in every play
and hounds her teachers, who respond, *We'll see.*
But cast as Rudolph's Wife, The Month of May,
a snail, and Aesop's mouse, respectively,

no wonder she feels cheated, like her plan
is meaningless, her squeaky voice unheard,
and asked to choose a brave American
she writes her book report on Larry Bird.

So her persistence tends to go unseen
as when she hides under the bathroom sink
for upwards of an hour, fetal between
the ratty towels and hotel soaps, the pink

sponge rollers, even though—*ready or not*—
they're not. Imagine her surprise, emerging
from her mildewed chrysalis (the perfect spot)
to find her friends have quit, frustration verging

on something sinister. She senses this
and tempers her reply with dignified
indifference; thus, her hypothesis:
it's best nobody knows how hard you tried.

She reinvents herself, adopts the skills
most suited to the settings she observes,
and though relieved when—finally!—she fills
her lanky frame, hatching war-worthy curves,

she's stricken with misgivings. Has she missed
the point? *Bildungsroman*? Routine progression,
whereby the foundling, insurrectionist
or ordinary child achieves accession

into the ordinary sphere? Perhaps,
yet with each step our heroine must find
the least resistant path and close the gaps.
Such posturing requires she leave behind

her first hermetic world, the seamless id,
and by the time, nostalgic, she admits
she's ready to return, the former kid
contortionist, of course, no longer fits.

II.

THE SCHOOL BY THE ZOO

The world goes by my cage and never sees me.

—Randall Jarrell

I. Big Sandstone Building in Memory of

Preparing for the future, slow and steady,
the students cruise these traveled halls with ease.
Some will concede to genius—when they're ready;
for now, it's hard enough to find a seat
or hear the expert on Diogenes
(required). Meanwhile, the fledgling *corps d'elite*,
will idle, limacine, along the quad
and rehearse Real Life, Act One: the smile-and-nod.

Others, like *fish* or *deer*, will reify
a pluralistic singularity:
upstairs, a girl who charts the blinking I
between the margins of the screen—her mind
racing to keep her place—works constantly,
fidgets, deletes, and realigns, resigned
to making notes for notes she ought to keep;
she pencils in her planner *wake up, sleep.*

II. *Ecce Signum!*

Billboards all over town forecast the news,
foreshortened, *Giant Pandas Coming Soon!*
And though they didn't come, devoted crews
pressed on and met the necessary quotas,
unfazed by phantom deadlines, *April... June...*
It went unsaid, erecting faux pagodas,
a gift shop, and Asian species carousel:
the deal with China wasn't going well.

Come August, though, fresh off the aestivation,
a boy reporter for the campus rag
will pen a feature on the situation—
between an op-ed ("Mothering Iraq")
and black-and-white cartoons of deans in drag.
But football's in the air. The campus clock
falls back, and local color's lost on fans
who flock to sports bars, making better plans.

III. Involution

The concrete matrix of the dorm confirms
her lie: *I'll meet you there.* She never does,
fifth wheel, or third; in algebraic terms,
expressionless, an X without a Y.
The girl knows *some* line intersects (is, was),
the point she's lost, or can't identify—
but nonce sense is the method she evolves,
creating problems solving never solves.

She thinks her trouble lies in being born
straddling two astral signs, Virgo and Libra,
a virgin tipped off-balance. Thus, she's torn
between the standard (beating a dead horse)
and deviation (…or a mule, or zebra).
Rephrased: tautologies, a onetime source
of consolation, leave her none the wiser.
She is her only factor, and divisor.

IV. Swan Song

The post-game party thrives. They roast a hog,
burnt offering to honor pigskin gods
who haven't shown. All night, an underdog
mentality unites the Sigma Phis
with bones to pick. "Who's that, the practice squad's
third string? Big deal..." Of course, none signifies
the wild drive to "suck out all the marrow"
like a barebacked senior in a red sombrero.

It stirs the siamangs, his blunt, staccato
rhythm: he's stoned, moonlighting on the drums.
The distant stare, the tribalist bravado...
"Didn't he make All-Conference freshman year?"
"You're a *natural*," his parents (both alums)
had urged, fueling a long, sidelined career
(best of the also-rans). What lengths we'll go
in order not to hear "I told you so."

V. *Dramatis Personae*

The understudy cuts up, impromptu
sketch comedy as ritual effacement:
BLOW ME. Who wants to play Gravedigger 2,
upstaged in one scene? (*To soliloquize
or act out…*) Yet the Prince (textbook displacement,
antic disposition) has butterflies
and night sweats; by rehearsals, *freaking out*,
he'll flee the whips and scorns of showtime doubt.

That undiscovered country, the other side,
lies always just beyond what none can see
beyond—alas, a self-composed divide:
just as ape artists paint a cage with bars,
players project their angst, decide to be
rebels (or critics? Countless escritoires
bear names and numbers etched among their scrawls:
FOR A GOOD TIME CALL ___. Nobody calls).

VI. Interiors

Enter Miss Running Mouth who exercises
freedom of speech. A budding libertine
aesthete, her right brain (Fine Arts) analyzes
feng shui relationships through spectral-cues:
the common room's chartreuse and billiard green
pick up her Solo cup and leopard shoes
to breed a kind of *art de cirque* decor,
a la some lost Lautrec—and she's the whore.

No really, it's okay. She says it, too;
she used to be a bookworm, insecure,
the bride of quietness, and then she grew
impatient. "Every heroine just needs
a *lyric legion.* Don't be so demure,
you know?" She thumbs her pearls like abacus beads
as if to score the herd of doting boys
she's charmed (*still* talking), paramour of noise.

VII. Offices

Daylight. Ascending from the sunken stacks,
the PolySci professor has the bends.
He rounds the quad, but autochthonous packs
of doe-eyed coeds, skirts like icing roses,
distract him. *Could it be their fate depends*
upon the surface layers a dress exposes?
Unfathomable... Lost in lust, he's struck
upside the head. A Frisbee. Just his luck.

It's moving day. After a storied reign,
he'll reassess his view of ivory towers
from underground (the imminent domain).
Lacking a niche in gothic architecture,
he locks the door and holds, with office hours,
a grudge. For what's a life, a keynote lecture?
A book, co-authored? Hard work won't atone
the higher-ups' decision—set in stone.

VIII. "The monkeys make sorrowful noises overhead"

Moss grows. Plums rot. The howlers squabble on
and off like sirens. Apoplectic birds.
The desk says *I was here, but now I'm gone...*
A clue? Perhaps, but manic, pseudocidal,
the girl has no idea (her father's words)
whether she's lost a mare or found a bridle.
What now? she thinks. The only song they know
bursts from the Primate House, fortissimo.

She's stuck. An ambered fly. A bowl-shaped fish,
or else the bowl, her murkiest concerns
spreading like culture in a petri dish.
Still, lonely has two poles—part cure, part curse
(see *pharmakon*); between them, stasis turns
her room into a fine-tuned universe.
So locomotion's neither here nor there:
the *axis mundi* is her rolling chair.

IX. "I've been to the zoo. I said, I've been to the zoo"

Like brown banana-peels, the lizards sunning
are unremarkable, without a placard
to announce their phylum, background, something stunning
by which they'll be distinguished. So it goes
while people make the rounds; drawn to the lacquered
and overblown, they stand in line to pose
as bears and hippos, 2-D scenery
with cutout circles where the head should be.

Weekdays are free for students. Cooped-up labs
disperse, collecting data. Sculpture classes
crouch over drawing boards like pensive crabs
and capture animals in silhouette
or stretched synecdoches. In part, the zoo
provides escape: most visitors forget
their humdrum lives—an unrelenting plot
they're destined to remember they forgot.

X. Perspectives

The tour bunny—"Who here's a music whiz?"—
recites the script she memorized last spring;
all ears, the parents prod. "*You are*... He is!"
"You *are*," she echoes, coy decoy, her plan
to lead the pack right past the fine-arts wing
and flooded dorm (warped desks, procrustean
twin bunks in heaps)—*eyesores* would contradict
Endowment. Cutting edge. Top-ranked. Handpicked.

"Ahead..." An aimless fanfare, *au trompette*,
deadens her pitch. "...some dogwoods. To your right,
one of the founding deans posed with his pet
bloodhound." As more horns blare, a tough routine,
she stops to rub its muzzle. "On this site
they dedicated..." Sights set high, the dean
extends a stone arm toward the greater quarry
of his eponymous conservatory.

XI. Shaping Behaviors

The gym rats, up at dawn to circuit train,
watch CNN, but orange alerts and scenes
of hi-def wreckage roll right past. *No pain,
no gain*: they've hit their zone. Some set the pace,
some raise the bar. Their bodies are *machines*
and need upkeep to keep up with the race.
Besides, they've learned upkeep's its own reward—
better, in fact, than what they're racing toward.

Conditioning starts early: pint-sized Nikes,
then Gatorade and Wheaties. "Be like Mike"
(a more sophisticated taste than Mikey's
or Mickey's) sends the message "Don't be weak."
So runts set out—by stationary bike
or treadmill—striving for a cut physique,
a change protracted, chest hair to growth spurt,
each pitchy voice insisting, "Didn't hurt."

XII. Women's Studies

From boyfriends, dreamier than Irish setters,
to kiss-lock bags, pain pills, and debutante
genderlect ("Love ya lots" in bubble letters),
history is just an afterthought.
Stunning, how these façades of nonchalant
facility (laboriously wrought)
elude the eye. Like one of Rubin's vases,
a double-take shows two opposing faces.

Work hard, play hard; in time they'll reconcile
both *modi operandi*, sublimate
their baser faculties in Old World style.
Then, garnished with Phi Beta Kappa keys,
they'll stand in line, either to graduate
or register (Masters and PhDs),
and spend the years that follow making sure
nobody knows the kind of girls they were.

XIII. Ichnology

Hypothesis: research will never patch
the rift between deductions and unknowns.
Alone, the lab tech's notes, in chicken scratch,
go downhill (college-ruled into unruly)—
he'd hoped for temples, giant raptor bones,
a tunnel to boyhood's *Ultima Thule.*
In practice, *he* feels like the missing link,
drawing stick figures in archival ink.

It's late (even downstairs he hears the apes),
and sorting evidence of evidence
of prehistoric life—footprints and scrapes,
burrows and coprolites—he can't explain
its origins, much less its relevance.
Epochs of pressure form one marbled vein;
the afterimage of receding glaciers
a *tabula rasa*, record of erasures.

XIV. Ichthyology

…Or eschatology? (So many schools
to get them straight is an –ology itself.)
The girl, subjected to each subject's rules
(interpellated), must interpolate
a master narrative. And while her shelf
is stratified with spines that indicate
she likes the thought of being thought a thinker,
she falls for *someday soon* (hook, line, and sinker).

What next? What then? Between these old refrains
being becomes conditional to tense.
Thoughts rise like bubbles, but her mind remains
heavy. (*Cogito…*) Someday she'll have made
(the future perfect) *it*, at last, make sense.
For now, neology explains her trade—
logosasphyxiation (n): the act
of drowning in the sense one sought, but lacked.

XV. Reciprocity

To *give back* (philanthropic Greeks adopt
a stray or highway; independents tend
to picket things, while optimists co-opt
a neater politics— ☮ ❤ —in chalk;
likewise, with grants, the FCA can send
a team to China and later fund a talk
on China) means both knowing what to save
and showing what you got from what you gave.

Though each club seems auspicious at the start,
a *sui generis* menagerie,
the most committed set themselves apart
by plugging on. The rest, like fabled hares,
soon lose the plot, or drive (major: Ennui).
Does patience pay? Just ask the millionaires
who stood, years later, braving April's rain
while pandas landed in a private plane.

XVI. *Mutatis Mutandis*

Spring finals, fast approaching last resorts,
the annual staff attaches party pics
and portraits. Facing past-due lab reports
or themes left undeveloped, they lack focus,
so shots from Formal Week are marked "Forensics,"
no-shows moved lower on the totem (*locus
desperatus*) than freshmen, misspelled names
floating like driftwood under empty frames.

Not pictured: dark rooms where evasive species
scratch at the surface, hoping they'll surmount
the past's supreme italic. Though their theses
and specimen may aid them (*floruit*
in progress), seeing as it's hard to count
among one's errors failing to submit
(c.f. the girl I was), they rearrange
the things they've saved, expecting things to change.

III.

TACTICS: A SHORT LESSON

I. Mimicry

Regarding threat, responses
rarely vary; *fight or flight*, you've heard—
yet, overlooked, self-fashioning
offers a third resort:
become (as such) the thing the thing
pursuing you won't touch.

Or rather, *seem* to, seeming
being key, for even maquillage
requires a sharper artifice
to forge (what else?) a spot-on
forgery—so *notice this*
eclipses *notice me*.

II. Crypsis

Others would rather try
a guise of shadow, stripes, or shape in flux
between two optic opposites
(like certain birds with getups
tailor-made from counterfeits
of shade and countershade).

In contrast, monochrome
supports a masquerade of subtleties
so those who stalk the *tertium quid*
will pass, failing to see
the lacewing queen or katydid
for all the forest's green.

III. Idem

Well, have I lost you yet?
I'm coy, I know, but don't mind being chased
as long as you're two steps behind—
it's just sometimes *approach*
feels like *attack* and, found, I find
I want my background back.

But hell, long as we're here,
alone, together, intimate seems nice—
honest. Excusing oversights,
I'm honest more or less,
an open book. Just dim the lights
so I can change. Don't look.

PORTRAIT OF THE ARTIST
WITH PAINT-BY-NUMBERS

"Every Man a Rembrandt!"
—Palmer Paint advertisement (1951)

Of humble provenance—a hobby shelf,
a shrink-wrapped box—my paintings strive for pith
and insight, though the presentation falls
a few strokes shy of beauty: The Old Estate
with Hounds. Big Top. Midnight on Mount Rainier.
This week, it's Umpteenth Beach. An accident
of symmetry, enormous dorsal fins
mirror a V of Vs. Adjacent breakers
refuse to break; skiffs sail across the border,
all headed west. And while it isn't *good*—
too uniform, too plumb—unlikelihood
seems perfectly portrayed by perfect order.
If every man's a Rembrandt, this scene's makers
have made things easier. The work begins
when, having seen the ending, I'm content
to use their template. Not much changes here.
I picture days unnumbered but create
idylls of idleness, my proof these walls
necessitate the art I fill them with,
an imitation only of itself.

SVENGALI DECK

With this pack, this dream of magicians is now realized.
—Burling Hull, Instruction Sheets

Lately, it's come to blows,
and some may fear our end is nearing—
tomatoes, airhorns: fans are disappearing,
resentful of the hyped, high-priced admissions,
the Master So and So's. Magicians,
    those dog and pony shows

you're pushing won't distract
a Doubting Thomas, well aware
that once the pyrotechnics lose their flair,
you'll cue some dry ice, frantic violins,
or Act Two's deconstructed twins,
    stage right—*voilà*: intact—

in flesh-toned leotards
(one Marilyn, one vintage Britney).
Likewise, they've seen your Now You See It litany,
its hocus-pocuses inconsequential
as top hats bearing exponential
    rabbits or linked foulards—

so ditch the overkill.
For, of our switcheroos and sleights,
or layings on, of hands, the sudden flights
of pigeons—all the shticks we've bought or sold—
none does the trick quite like the old
    illusion of free will.

Svengali knew this well,
and in his name I've built a pack
that's guaranteed to bring the magic back

to Magic, timeless subterfuges
where spectators become the stooges,
    convinced you've cast a spell.

    The truth is, in this age
of reproduction, we make do
by making stock routines look new, and true
to form, my deck will trump your favorite props,
cutting sunk costs and bellyflops
    as, spotlit, you assuage

    even the self-professed
hotshots. It's endlessly amusing
to watch the Chosen One assume he's choosing
a random card—nobody gets the part
that's in the cards: his royal heart
    is just like all the rest.

PLOT TWISTS

They hammer roses over bolted doors
and speak in code of loopholes, hidden strings.
With spells, they overwrite the hex. They trace
their genealogy from famous kings
to geniuses. They settle ancient scores,
bid traitors clipped, and bag the leggy spy.
They spread their wealth with giant cardboard checks,
    and more than once they chase
    a guy who's not their guy.

Reconnaissance takes months. They're issued masks
and parachutes, then paired with doppelgangers.
They're trained to practice tactics of remote
control and, housed in unmarked airplane hangars,
they finalize their plan, assigning tasks
to teams. They study fate and husbandry
and rear the beasts of rotten luck: gift horses
    Charley horses, the goat
    behind Door #3.

They say, *We said we'd save your village, true,*
but when we said we serve the greater good,
we lied—we couldn't help it. They explain
hamartia (they feel misunderstood).
The thing is, we would never target you.
We love civilians. See? Our guns are fake.
This proves to be a minor consolation,
    like extra Novocain,
    or cookies at a wake.

Outrage ensues. Their base and fancy camps
are toppled. *Like the walls of Jericho!*
they shout—about the time the shouting stops,
and in the silence, locusts come and go.
They check their schedules; renegades and tramps

emerge from musty grottos, bellicose
and closing in. As *if* gives way to *when*
    the sky rumbles and drops.
    They say, *Well, adios.*

And in the end, they tell their sons they won,
a fate sealed in the laudatory strophes
of *What a Run They Had* (a group of odes).
They potpourri their laurels, case their trophies
with other trophies, adding, *That was fun,*
then join the shadowed figures—sleepy, sore—
who nod off watching their respective Zeniths
    while the living room explodes
    with someone else's war.

FLEA CIRCUS

A vision of persistence, this ringmaster
        outshines other hawkers.
        Heralding his grand
minutiae, he's fine-tuned the ballyhoo

that woos us, dazed, up to the hotbox stage
        where pairs of tightropes quiver
        over flaming hoops.
We squint when he unlids a jar and frees

his headline act: Amelio the Great
        whose gravity-defying
        troupe of trapeze dames
will dangle from the bar, hooked teeth to toes,

until they're launched across the hippodrome
        as wee cabriolets
        with fourteen-karat spokes
are raced by seven Herculean sons.

Or so we're told. The whir of turning wheels
        remains our only proof
        this company exists
but scatters, acrobatic, between blinks

and double-takes. Fair-weather audience,
        we crane and strain to hear
        a muted song, off key.
What fingers plink that slight calliope?

Convinced the show's a hoax, we'll go home mad,
        but prickling with an itch
        that teases us to ask,
without the fleas, how could there be a circus?

FELIX CULPA

Without a hitch, the ice cream maker churns
in whirling jerks that shake the mirrored tray
of geometric cheese and crudités.
Another bride-to-be stands clueless—*Blessed*,

she says, thanking her hosts, who take the hint
and raise their glasses. It's good company
save for no-see-ums and humidity,

nothing they can't survive. With funeral fans
and empty cones, they crowd the patio
like a life raft, concurrent conversations
adrift in genteel reconciliations—
Let's get together sometime. Out front, groups

of subdivision kids retrace their loops
around the cul-de-sac. Most sacrifice
control for speed and flout the good advice
of partygoers—*careful!*—who don't know

a prank will overturn their evening plans:
they lean on the verisimilitude
of a table held with half its screws unscrewed,
the rest clinking like milk money with lint

inside the prankster's pocket—she, a guest
of guests, who's looking forward to the crash
and unicycles past with crack panache,
ecstatic that the ice cream maker churns.

EPITHALAMIUM

Weddings, she thinks she's getting good at them,
she says. You bet. Except maybe she pulled
a muscle—that bouquet weighed twenty pounds,

or something, didn't it? It did. Bouquets,
big ones, can up the ambience as far
as weddings go. Sometimes it's hard to stand

so still without locking your knees, without
not thinking, *Smile. Don't lock your knees.* She says,
and what about the band? The compote? Mint,

she says, is great, but tends to dominate;
ask anyone with mint. But great. She says,
I'm good at weddings; call me Mustang Sally.

Five bridesmaids by the pool. The pool is closed,
and fenced in, though they've hopped the fence to sit
with stemware, cards, no towels, playing a game

where someone gets to be the president.
You've got mascara there and there, they say.
She's good at this, mascara notwithstanding.

So what my dress is ruined. Right? she says.
So what about my shoes, I hate those shoes,
hey, can't we play again. And they agree

it's buggy by the pool. The deck gets wet,
cards stick together. Doesn't chlorine stink?
I'm Tammy Faye, she says, watching a spider—

which might be just an insect, this depends
whether or not two legs are antennae,
locate a shadow. Disappear. She says,

I'm *sure* I pulled a muscle, and she did:
after the ceremony, when they flung
those bowling balls of roses—all of them—

into the hotel trash. Lovely bouquets,
but no one needs a dying carry-on.
Among them she's the oldest, tied for shortest,

barefoot, without a towel. They've eaten me
alive, she says. I'm positive. They say,
then go, we dare you, but she doesn't go,

having remembered she misplaced, or lost,
her shoes, forgetting that she doesn't care
who wins. Call me Miss Sisyphus, she says.

STORM AND STRESS

That a spider web supports a bead of rain
    is as significant
as rain's resolve, poised where some spinneret
    has pitched its threads aslant,
since, held or holding, each endures a strain—
    one presses, one reacts.
Don't ask me what it's worth. Despite the facts
    of matter's favored states,
such concentration's of no consequence
    beyond this life, a net
tailored to break, too late for recompense
    when weight evaporates.

AFTERMATH

Those who were standing experienced sensations of dizziness &
vertigo. Several ladies who were sitting complained that they felt
as if sitting on a poise, and were afraid of falling from their seats.
In an upper chamber, something suspended from the wall was
observed to flip sensibly against it.
　　　　　　　　　　—The York Gazette, *January 24, 1812*

Well, so much for the get-together. Heads
　　can catch the drifts of continents—
strange latitudes. But once the center shifts

we lean—Atlas and Axis—on some conjured
　　Morse or psalm, for history
has proved, with just a bit of tweaking, calm

becomes calamity. The thought alone
　　will flush your cheeks. We're wired to blame
freak accidents, yet ridicule the freaks

who worry over vagaries—anthrax
　　or shark attacks—stockpiling mace,
hand-sanitizer, first aid fannypacks,

for nose to nose with bathroom mirrors, all
　　we see is blur. We say "we" meaning
"I" because we're never really sure

we're not alone. At root, the aftermath
　　(or *second mowing*) just confirms
our vertigo: we stop; the world keeps going.

Thus, seasoned, we learn not to trust new growth
　　or solid ground: when Mother Nature
runs her course, she dishes out a round

of scratch disasters—twisters, pumpkin floods,
     a deadly freeze; her sucker punch
can bring colossal statues to their knees.

Still standing? Then we're soon exposed to shots
     that turn the mind (a *camera
obscura*) upside down. In time, we find

it's just a matter of perspective: first
     one side gets hit. The other side,
then, from some numb remove, gets wind of it

—until a later breaking story ("Elsewhere
     Torn Asunder!") stirs the wake
of what's just broken. Is it any wonder

we've grown to need concinnity (shut doors
     and even planes, and noise to tune out
other noise), and though our ceiling stains

turn yellow-brown like ancient maps, we don't
     address the leak that drips (*dit-dah*)
in pots and pans. Left with the shakes, we'll speak

louder, resolved to keep our cool and buttressed
     by pretending: diffidence
dressed up as poise—that old feminine ending.

For once we've dodged the storm or tremors, spooked
     but seeking closure, we'll insist
that it was nothing, feigning gained composure

like ladies—*My!*—who straighten chairs or wind
     the frazzled clocks, while upstairs
in an empty room, an empty cradle rocks.

DEAD MATTER

When neon ginkgoes fan the window panes
and sycamores unroll their yellow sleeves,
when rust moves through the maple's palmate veins
and tulip poplars blush with spade-shaped leaves,
when spruces shoot umbrellas, glued in twos,
where purple beeches bifurcate and twist,
when catkins crack and ivy wraps the yews,
a cold-snap snaps, abruptly ends the list.

Then pomp and pigment peel like painters' rags,
reduced to heaps of dirt. Long past their prime,
our fruits of labor steep in garbage bags.
We haul them off, the waste of wasted time—
for all forms wilt with mildew, blight, disease.
This guy I used to love studied the trees.

ASSISTED LIVING

I.

They bring her gladiolas, macaroons.
She hardly looks up from the scarf she knits,
her shoulders like a hanger in her blouse.
The children join her, fidgeting (they're hot),
and when she snaps, *You're late,* the father vows
to be more patient—as if this acquits
a history of ruined afternoons.

She says the schedule's rotten (whist, mahjong).
Her liver spots are spreading. Sunday's roast
was stiff as shingles, and the walls make noise
(one neighbor knocks; one strolls, a bath-robed ghost).
"But what a view," they say. It won't be long.

II.

She thanks them for the overpriced bouquet,
the sweets, which added to the stack will go
untouched. Sure as the world. *A crying shame
you never visit me*, she tells the boys,
calling the oldest by his brother's name.
They nod. "Mmm-hmm, yes ma'am," and make the slow
procession to the parlor. *Can't you stay*

for supper? "Oh," the father says, "the drive…"
stopping to watch the man from 3-B pour
his water bottle in the wicker pot
of a silk ficus. *Fool's been told before,*
she mutters. *Thinks he's keeping it alive.*

MINIATURES

They tell you everything goes back
to childhood, as if you could
fathom that prelapsarian world
packed in the basket of your first
banana seat 1-speed, crack it
like a buckeye and pick the meat
of what you saw through the fourth wall
you crouched by. Tidy latticework
and shutters hid the inside's lack

of baths and stairs and, troubled, you
shifted the shower stall from room
to room with too much furniture—
sealed wardrobes, chests of empty drawers.
And worse, the family didn't mesh:
one older child, a daughter/son
in knickers melted flush with flesh;
one baby like a swaddled raisin,
abducted from some snowy crèche.

Why would the cookware set include
a tub of Crisco, colander,
and gravy boat—no knives or spoons?
And what about the escritoire,
its little green glass banker's lamp
without a battery or cord,
only a filamentless bulb?
Like any kid, you only wanted
stories uniformly built—

that's why you made the collie stay
guarding the hearth; her master, trapped
inside the flue, had learned the flue
was not a suction chute. Dislodged,
he lounged before the gramophone,
wishing for feet instead of shoes.

Meanwhile, the eunuch broke a horse
and split, and mother washed her hands
of all their monkey business. Pissed

at the sheer impossibility
of dinner, she soon parked herself
behind the wheel of a stolen jeep,
pressing against the hollow where
the horn should be, resolved that once
her infant vaulted off the roof
she'd rev the engine, clearing yards
of carpet—if she had to drive
all night, they'd find a goddamn Shoney's.

THE TRUTH ABOUT DISTANCE

Now, of course, Newton, when he spoke of the distance, meant the distance at a given time: he thought there could be no ambiguity about time. But we have seen that this was a mistake.
—Bertrand Russell

Her unicycle's parked down in the basement,
    a dusty souvenir she stows
    with antiques, out-of-fashion clothes.
She hasn't ridden since the hip replacement,

except in sleep, but this will have to do.
    Her doctor says, Why push your luck?
    She shrugs, tallies another duck
that won't stay in its row. (It's nothing new.)

Her tightrope rides replaced with strong black tea,
    she reads the Living Section twice
    (Miss Manners, Abby, seem so nice
when they become your only company),

and there's no looking forward since she's grieving
    the three dead aunts she never met,
    plus kudzu, crosswords, long-term debt,
and all the mail she hasn't been receiving.

She hates to nag the postman, but insists
    one shouldn't leave old business pending,
    convinced *this time* the world is ending,
a claim the neighborhood psychologists

present as further proof she's full of beans,
    Cassandra in a dressing gown
    who never pulls her nightshades down,
a whirl of fabric flapping as she cleans.

She takes her pensions to the bingo hall
    (O-86? *Oh, 86,*
    the flood of numbered days) and picks
more cards than she can count, loses them all,

then goes home, weeps into her fine bone cup,
    exciting storms of Darjeeling.
    (What torrents loneliness can bring...)
Ah well, she says. At least her heart rate's up.

Of course, these platitudes won't curb the doubt,
    a chill that lifts her silver hairs
    and draws her to the basement stairs
until she wheels the unicycle out

and wipes the cobwebbed spokes, or thumbs a scuff,
    and gives the rusty wheel a spin,
    and thinks, *I was fantastic then,*
and sometimes (Lord have mercy) that's enough.

A CORRELATED HISTORY OF SYNCHRONICITY

According to those who say they see it, the face, with deepset eyes, beard, and crown of thorns, is on a billboard advertising Pizza Hut spaghetti.

—The Commercial Appeal, *Memphis, TN*

It's happening everywhere, this *surely not…*
crop circles, sages, spacemen, crooked fruit,
recurring phrases, yetis, Nessies, Elvis.
From Nashville's famous "Nun Bun" (folded dough
slathered with raisin glaze that somehow favors
Mother Teresa) to the Jesus weeping
on oaks in Natchitoches, we've seen it all,
bewildered witness to our own desires.
We nurse a need for order, patterns, webs
of information, perfect gyres, The Law

of Truly Large Numbers, and could we trace
time back to our obscene gelatinous start,
perhaps we'd find the missing helices.
But that won't stop the Georgia divorcée
who, with the poise of bygone martyrs, swore
to god and Channel Five her truth appeared
in marinara eyes. And that won't stop
the motorists who heard the news and followed,
cocksure they'd prove her right, the demipilgrims
with their hymns and glowing votives, asking "Here?"

"Or here?" or me, my grandma three weeks gone,
the way I reeled through Dublin's side streets, trailing
her thick familiar scent of Estée Lauder,
compelled to chase its owner up the glazed
cathedral steps, as if I'd find her there,
as if there is a method to the nothing
behind our opened doors, our rolled-back stones.

Someone was vacuuming the Lady Chapel,
and so I waited in a vacant pew,
hoping, with patience, ordinary shapes

would rise like dust above the slope of light,
and I kept waiting. This was years ago,
but I'm no wiser for the time, alone
with nervous systems, threads unraveling
inside a room I haven't left all day
despite the city going dark behind
my window in this multi-storied complex,
curator of coincidence, high priestess
of sense in absentia—perplexed to recognize
my own face glossed across the passing world.

Praise for Previous Winners of the Vassar Miller Prize in Poetry

Stray Home, by Amy M. Clark:

Two poems from *Stray Home* were selected by Garrison Keillor, host of *A Prairie Home Companion* and of *The Writer's Almanac* to be included in *The Writer's Almanac*, broadcast May 28 and 29, 2010.

"*Stray Home* is a great read. The poetic form found in its pages never feels forced or full of clichés. Whether you are a fan of formal verse or just like to 'dabble,' *Stray Home* is a collection to pick up."—*Good Reads*

Ohio Violence, by Alison Stine:

"In the mind, Ohio and violence may not be words immediately paired—pastoral cornfields, football fields, and deer versus the blood and splintered bone of a fight or a death. Yet *Ohio Violence* achieves that balance of the smooth and vivid simmer of images and the losses that mount in Alison Stine's collection."—*Mid-American Review*

"Shot through with a keen resolve, *Ohio Violence* is an arresting, despairing book that alternately stuns and seduces."—*Rain Taxi*

"One comes away from *Ohio Violence* newly impressed with the contingency and instability of the hazardous universe that is our home; and impressed, as well, with the ability of these stark, memorable poems to distill that universe into language and to make of it a sad and haunting song."—Troy Jollimore, *Galatea Resurrects #13*

Mister Martini, by Richard Carr:

"This is a truly original book. There's nothing extra: sharp and clear and astonishing. Viva!"—Naomi Shihab Nye, author of *Fuel*, judge

The Next Settlement, by Michael Robins:

"Michael Robins' prismatic poems open windows, then close them, so we're always getting glimpses of light that suggest a larger world. With never a syllable to spare, these poems are beautiful and haunting. I know of nothing like them."—James Tate, winner of the 1992 Pulitzer Prize for Poetry

"*The Next Settlement* is a finely honed, resonant collection of poems, sharp and vivid in language, uncompromising in judgment. The voice in this book is unsparing, often distressed, and involved in a world which is intrusive, violent, and deeply deceitful, where honesty and compassion are sought for in vain, and refuges for the mind are rare."—Anne Winters, author of *The Key to the City*, judge

re-entry, by Michael White:

"Michael White's third volume does what all good poetry does: it presents the sun-drenched quotidiana of our lives, and lifts it all into the sacred space of poetry and memory. He delights us with his naming, but he also makes us pause, long enough at least to take very careful stock of what we have. He makes us want to hold on to it, even as it trembles in the ether and dissolves."—Paul Mariani, author of *Deaths and Transfigurations*, judge

"Here is a book that explores the interplay between interior and exterior landscapes with such generous and beautifully crafted detail that readers will feel they are no longer reading these poems but living them."—Kathryn Stripling Byer, Poet Laureate of North Carolina 2005–2009

"In Michael White's latest opus, figure after figure emerge from chaotic ground of memory, such verdant upswellings an urgent music pressured up from deep wells before subsiding—high waterlines left in our wake to mark the turbulence of love's intractable flood." — Timothy Liu, author of *For Dust Thou Art*

The Black Beach, by J. T. Barbarese:

"*The Black Beach* constantly delights with its questing, surprising, and not-easily-satisfied imagination. But simultaneously it creates an exacting and exhilarating vision of 'God, the undoer that does.' The speaker who, in one poem, stands in the moment 'love/what is not,' is the same one who, in another poem, imagines 'the black beach of heaven where all desire/ is merged, twinned, recovered, braided, and set ablaze.'"—Andrew Hudgins, author of *Ecstatic in the Poison,* judge

"A dark brilliance shines in these honed, memorable poems of the human predicament: that of a sentient particle with a mind for the infinite. 'Looking for meaning/ the way radio waves sought Marconi,' Barbarese's restless imagination searches through the stations of the daily to the 'very end of the dial/ the static that never signs off,' and turns back to receive what we have, the 'lonely surprised heart/ shaken. . .'"—Eleanor Wilner, author of *The Girl with Bees in Her Hair*

"Barbarese has an uncanny ability to size up the urban scene, then hallow and harrow it. Putting his daughter on the local train for the city, he conjures up those who rode in the boxcars to the ovens. And, leaning over 'winged rot . . . glued . . . to shat-on grass' in a nearby park, he can think 'how beautiful,/ the hard frost had cemented/ what had lived to what never did.' He wins me over in poem after poem."—Maxine Kumin, author of *The Long Marriage*

Losing and Finding, by Karen Fiser:

"There are so many delights in this book, interpenetrated by so many losses. . . . She keeps her eye unflinchingly on 'the rough loving arms of this world,' even as she is buffeted about by it."—Lynne McMahon, judge

"From the searing heart of pain and patience come the transporting poems of Karen Fiser. Trust them. Treasure them. These poems are resounding, important, and deeply humane."—Naomi Shihab Nye, author of *Fuel*

Bene-Dictions, by Rush Rankin:

"*Bene-Dictions* is a canny, unnerving book. Its cool manners seem to hold compassion at bay; but its irony is a cleansing discipline which allows it to conjure complex lusts, hurts, and injustices without self-pity and, apparently, without delusion. These poems describe a world in which 'Tenderness is an accident of character/ or energy, or just a side-effect/ of having failed at what you wanted,' but in which the reader, to read the effect of rain on paper, 'opens the book/ in a storm, as though to find the world itself in tears.'"—Rosanna Warren, judge

"If the long hours in offices of the mind elect for us meaningfulness, they must always eventually find the human heart. Then Rankin's vivid and surprising poems map that movement where as Rilke insists, what is sublime is mundane, and everything that falls must somehow in shadow/act, rise."—Norman Dubie

The Self as Constellation, by Jeanine Hathaway:

"This is a collection to be read in sequence because the continuity is powerful and persuasive. If we are attentive readers, we end like the nuns in the storm cellar 'not knowing whether we've been struck by lightning or by love.'"—Madeline DeFrees, judge

The Perseids, by Karen Holmberg:

"It is a rare pleasure to encounter these days a young poet so thoroughly at home in the natural world, so deeply attuned to its mysteries, that reading her book we enter, in turn, that 'Spherical Mirror,' the elemental mind which, as *The Perseids* reminds us, forms 'the core of human bliss.'"—Sherod Santos, judge

A Protocol for Touch, by Constance Merritt:

"Merritt's prosodic range is prodigious—she moves in poetic forms as naturally as a body moves in its skin, even as her lines ring with the cadenced authority of a gifted and schooled ear. Here, in her words, the iambic ground bass is in its vital questioning mode: 'The heart's insistent undersong: how live? // how live? How live?' this poetry serves no lesser necessity than to ask that."—Eleanor Wilner, author of *The Girl with Bees in Her Hair* and judge

Moving & St rage, by Kathy Fagan:

"Kathy Fagan's long awaited second collection keeps revealing new strengths, new powers. Its words are of unsparing rigor; its intelligence and vision continually spring forward in changed ways. These are poems both revealing and resistant: deeply felt, deeply communicative, yet avoiding any easy lyricism. Again and again the reader pauses, astonished by some fresh turn of language, of insight, of terrain. *Moving & St rage* offers extraordinary pleasures, clarities, and depth."—Jane Hirshfield

"From the first emblems of language—the angular letters of A and K—a child steps toward the preservation of consciousness, and, in turn, the paradox of preserving that which is lost. These beautifully crafted poems trace a journey to adulthood and grief with a lyrical mastery that is breathtaking. *What can language do with loss?* Fagan asks. This splendid book is her answer."—Linda Bierds

Soul Data, by Mark Svenvold:

"*Soul Data* is rarely compounded—of wit and music, surface elegance and intellectual depth, quirk and quandary. Its sensual intelligence is on high alert, and the sheer unsheerness of its language—all its densities and textures—is a linguiphiliacal delight. Unmistakably American (the poetry's occasions and its cadences alike serve for signature) it has the jinx-meister's humors about it. A fine rhetorical savvy, in a mind inclined to the chillier depths: among poetic gifts these days it's an uncommon conjunction, a gift of mysteries, like the sight (across a night pond's surface) of bright-blue shooting star: one hopes the other humans get to see it."—Heather McHugh

American Crawl, **by Paul Allen***:*

"It is absolutely no exaggeration to say that no one is writing like Paul Allen. There is not an ounce of flab in his poems, which are informed by an urgency, a sense of personal commitment, and a passion rarely seen in contemporary poetry. America in the 1990s is not a comfortable world in which to live; and Paul Allen is certainly not the man to entertain us with fanciful invitations to dens of innocence. Though *American Crawl* is a first book, there is nothing jejune about the poems, or about the unique imagination that creates them. The publication of this book is an important contribution to American letters."—Richard Tillinghast, author of *The New Life*

The Sublime, **by Jonathan Holden***:*

"*The Sublime* embodies a poetry that is personal and public, and shows through clear-cut imagery how varied our imagined and actual lives are. Everything seems to be woven into this ambitious collection: love, war, divorce, fear, anger, doubt, grace, beauty, terror, popular culture, nature. This poetry challenges us to remain (or become) whole in an increasingly fragmented world."—Yusef Komunyakaa, judge

Delirium, **by Barbara Hamby***:*

"Barbara Hamby is an extraordinary discovery! A poet of compassion and elegance, she is a poet whose debut in *Delirium* promises a rich (and enriching) lifelong project."—Cynthia Macdonald

Partial Eclipse, **by Tony Sanders:**

"Sanders brings together his own sensibility (quizzical, approaching middle-age, slightly disaffected, bemused, learned but not stuffy) and an alertness to what can be appropriated from history, myth, the daily papers."—*Choice*

". . . a distinguished first collection from a poet about whom we will be hearing more."— *Houston Post*

"Sanders proceeds through his . . . poems with a pervasive steadiness of diction, . . . a syntactic resonance quite his own yet gratefully beholden to such exacting masters as Stevens and Ashbery. The freshness of the poems is a result of their immersion in life with others, achieving the resolute tonality of a man speaking not so much out or up but on, talking his way to the horizon."—Richard Howard, judge

CPSIA information can be obtained at www.ICGtesting.com
Printed in the USA
LVOW08s1410051214

417071LV00008B/7/P